Pearson Baccala...

Egypt's Greatest Treasure

Jane Langford

Benjay's sandals slid on the stone floor as he tried to match his father's long strides. The Pharaoh had finally decided to show his son the treasures that would one day be his. Benjay followed his father eagerly into the Treasure Room.

"Behold, my son," said the Pharaoh proudly, "you see before you the finest workmanship in the land."

Benjay gazed at the golden statues, the cedar wood furniture, the jewel-encrusted masks and baskets laden with precious gemstones: rubies, turquoise and lapis lazuli. Then he looked from the treasure, up into his father's eyes.

"Honorable father, these treasures are magnificent – but what is the most precious thing in all of Egypt?" he asked.

The Pharaoh laughed. "Oh, I could not answer that question, son! Ask your mother," he said. "She might know the answer. Her judgement in these matters is wise."

Benjay found his mother busy painting her eyes with the black kohl that emphasised her beauty.

"Oh wisest of mothers," he asked, "what is the most precious thing in the land?"

The Queen smiled at her son, "Why, you are, of course, Benjay!"

"No, not me, Mother!" said Benjay seriously. "I mean something that everyone in Egypt would consider to be valuable."

The Queen thought. "Perhaps you should ask the Grand Vizier," she said. "He is an extremely important man. He is sure to know the answer to your question."

Benjay entered the Great Hall of the Palace. The Grand Vizier stood surrounded by an earnest group of scribes.

"You must make a new inventory of all the Pharaoh's treasure," the Grand Vizier commanded. "These records are six months out of date!"

Benjay's eyes lit up. The Grand Vizier had a list of all the Pharaoh's treasure!

"Grand Vizier!" interrupted the Pharaoh's son. "As a man of wisdom, can you tell me what the most precious thing in the land is?"

The Grand Vizier bowed his head and considered the matter. Then he held up the long papyrus scroll that listed all the Pharaoh's treasures.

"Why, the scroll is the most precious thing in Egypt," he said. "Without scrolls we could not keep records of all the goods and people in the land. Such documents help us to govern the land."

The Grand Vizier led Benjay to the Pharaoh's library. It was filled with thousands upon thousands of neatly written scrolls. "The knowledge of a thousand lifetimes is written on these scrolls," said the Vizier. "Astronomy! Medicine! Geography! History! Law! Yes! The scroll is definitely the most precious thing in the land."

Benjay was taken aback. This was not the sort of answer that he had expected. He returned to his mother's room.

"Have you found the answer to your question?" asked the Queen.

"Yes," said Benjay dubiously, "but it was not the answer that I expected. Perhaps I should ask someone else?"

"Of course!" said the Queen. "Why don't you consult with one of the scribes? They are very wise men indeed!"

So Benjay hurried out of the room and went to find the scribes.

As Benjay walked down the corridor he heard voices echoing in the royal storerooms. He peered in and saw several scribes sitting amongst the bulging sacks of grain.

"What are you doing?" asked Benjay.

"Making a tally of all the grain in the royal storerooms, Your Highness," replied one scribe. "We had a good harvest last year."

Benjay surveyed the scribes with their scrolls and sighed. Just then the Chief Scribe arrived to check on his men.

"You look troubled, Your Highness," he exclaimed. "May I help?"

"I wish to know what the most precious thing in the land is," said Benjay. "I suppose you also think it is the scroll?"

"The scroll?" The Chief Scribe raised his eyebrow. "A scroll certainly has much value. But what is the use of a scroll without an instrument to write on it with?" The Chief Scribe held up his pen. "This is the most precious thing in the land."

Benjay looked at the pen in astonishment. It was just a single reed, shaped at the end so that it could be dipped into ink. It did not look very valuable!

Benjay thanked the Chief Scribe and went in search of his father.

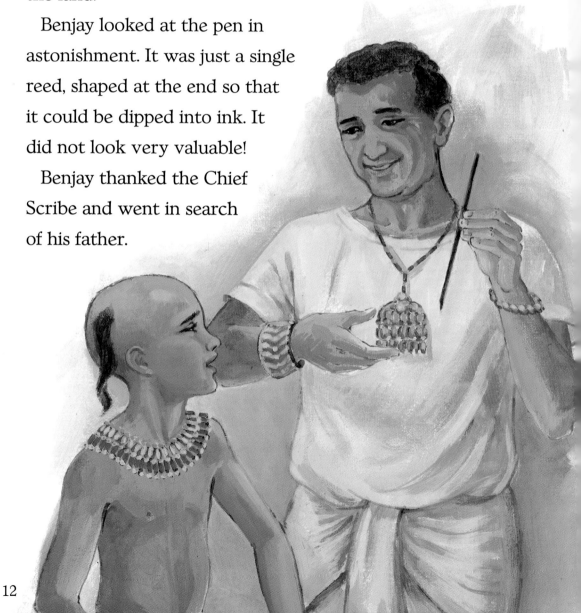

"What is the matter, son?" asked the Pharaoh. "Have you not found the answer to your question yet?"

Benjay shook his head, "Not the answer I am looking for," he replied.

"Come, let us go down to the river," said the Pharaoh. "You can ask the merchants. They bring precious goods to Egypt from countries far and wide."

"What a good idea!" exclaimed Benjay.

A merchant stood amongst the goods on his boat. The decks were crammed with crates of copper and ivory, jars of oil, baskets of exotic fruit and sacks of wheat.

Benjay smiled. This man would surely have the answer to his question.

"How may I help you, my lord?" the Merchant asked.

"I want to learn what the most precious thing in the land is," said Benjay.

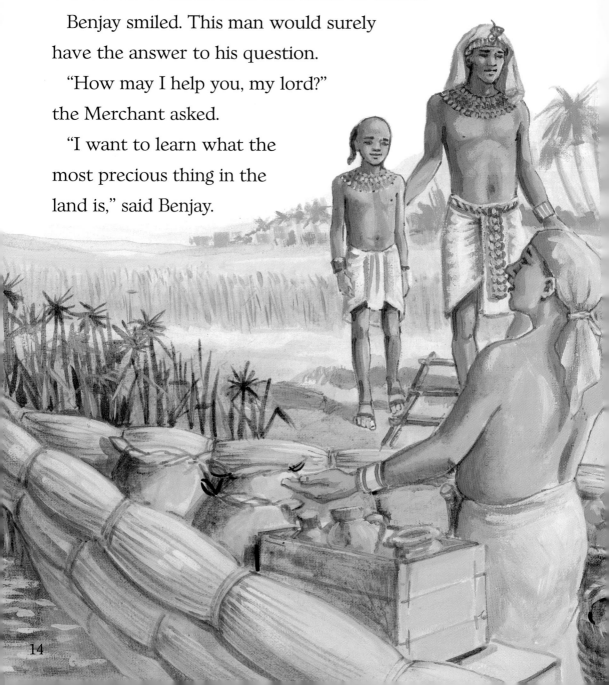

The merchant laughed heartily.

"That is simple," he said, "it is my boat!" He proudly patted the flimsy structure made from bundles of reeds. "Without it I could not travel the length of the River Nile. I could not bring back treasures from far away lands!"

Benjay beamed. A boat! That was a good answer. But then he frowned. A boat was certainly a valuable thing, but was it really the most precious thing in the land?

The Pharaoh summoned his son. "Come on, Benjay," he said, "I must visit the farmers. We need to ensure our people are well fed."

Benjay followed his father along the irrigation channels that fed the wheat fields with the water of the Nile. The Pharaoh stopped to greet a group of farmers. Benjay asked one of them his question.

"What do you consider to be the most precious thing in the land?" he asked.

"The most precious thing?" The farmer scratched his head. "I know what the most precious thing is to me. It is this bucket!"

He held up a reed bucket, blackened with tar to make it
waterproof.

"What do you use it for?" asked Benjay.

"Let me show you," said the farmer. He led Benjay to the
banks of the Nile and pointed to a strange device.

"We call this a shaduf," explained the farmer. "We use it to lift water. The bucket hooks onto the end of this pole. A clay weight hangs on the other end. I dip the bucket into the water like so... then I use the counter-weight to lift it back up, like so... Now I can pour the water into the irrigation channels."

Benjay looked at the shaduf in dismay. It certainly did not look precious, but he had to admit that it was yet another good answer. His head started to swim.

"Come," said the Pharaoh, "it is time we went home."

At the palace the Queen was awaiting Benjay's return. "Did you find the answer to your question?" she asked.

Benjay sighed, "No, Mother! The Grand Vizier says the most precious thing in the land is the scroll. The Chief Scribe believes it is the pen. The merchant thinks it is his boat and the farmer his bucket! How do I know which one is right?"

The Pharaoh mused over these answers. At last he spoke.

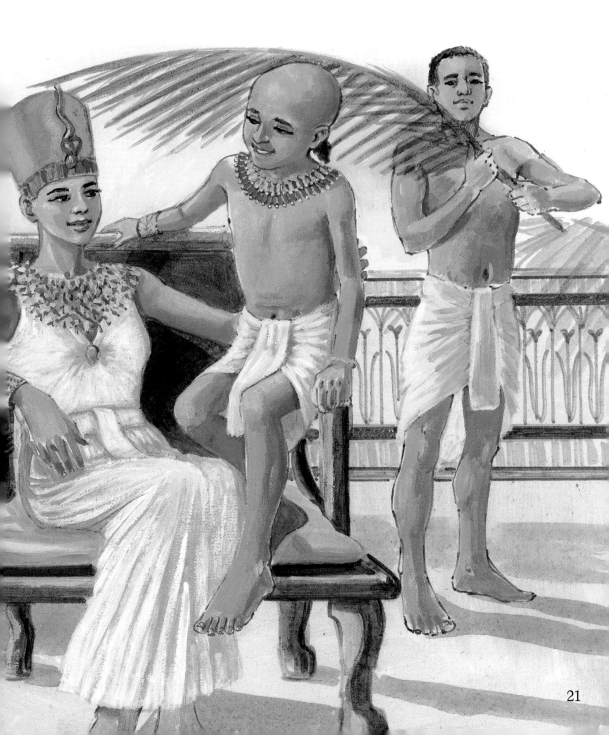

"What is the Grand Vizier's scroll made from?" he asked.

"Papyrus! The reeds that grow on the banks of the River Nile," answered Benjay proudly.

The Pharaoh nodded. "What is the Chief Scribe's pen made from?"

Benjay hesitated. "A reed – a papyrus reed from the riverbank."

The Pharaoh smiled. "What is the merchant's boat made from?" he asked.

Benjay smiled too. "Bundles of papyrus reed, tied together," he said.

"And finally," laughed the Pharaoh, "what is the farmer's bucket made from?"

"Reeds!" shouted Benjay. "They are all made from reeds!"

"So what is the most precious treasure in the land?" asked the Pharaoh.

"Papyrus reeds!" shouted Benjay.

"Correct!" declared the Pharaoh.

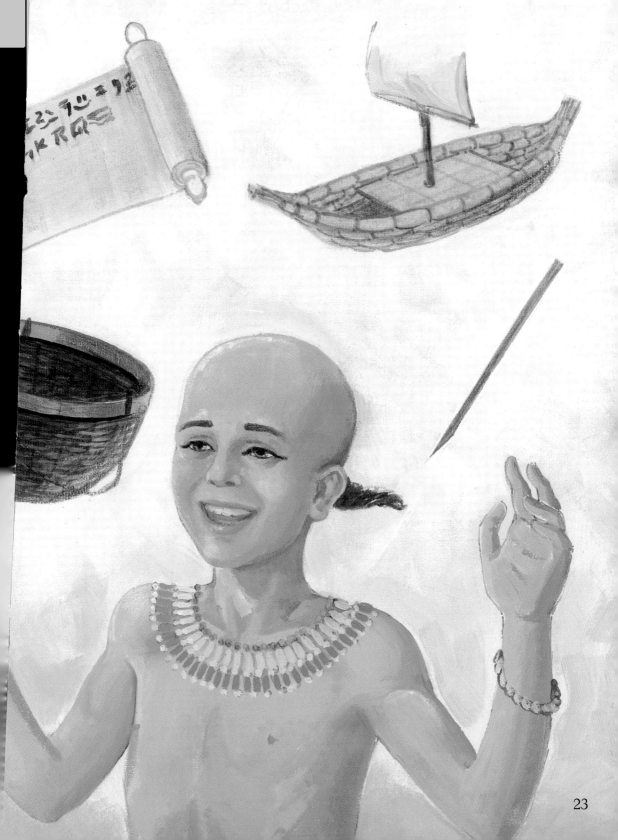

But the Queen shook her head.

"You are both mistaken," she said. "The most precious thing in the land of Egypt is the water of the River Nile. Where would your reeds grow if there were no water? What would any of us do without water, to drink and wash with and grow our crops? Consider that, when you talk of reeds!"

The Pharaoh smiled at his son.

"There you have your answer!" he said. "Your mother has proved her superior wisdom – once again!"